War
In The Name of
Beauty

by

Dylan Simon Alexander

DEDICATION

This book is dedicated to the inspired writings of Khalil Gibran, Rumi, Hafez and Paulo Coelho who are alchemists of Life on the voyage upon the lonely wild seas and stormy nights, and who have illuminated my Mind and Soul and turned my Heart into gold.

Their voice, passion, wisdom and spirit are echoed in the magnificence of the reader's imagination who lays their eyes upon their sacred writings and who opens their Heart to the profound beauty contained within the pages of their Soul.

A Prayer for the weak at Heart for strength and guidance.

To mother Earth for providing all the wisdom and nutrients to nourish the Mind, Body and Soul through which I have been able to write this book amongst the rivers, mountains, lakes and jungles, under the moonlight.

My He/Art. My true Teacher. Thank you for lighting the way to my Soul.

CONTENTS

"When the body is unattended to

The foundation of the temple is weak

When the mind is blind

The eyes are impotent

When the heart is clouded

Speech is futile"

- An ode to he who has seen the darkness in the battlefield between his heart's desires and his mind's illusions

***

"Words and actions have the power

To heal

Or to crush the human spirit

Be an "encourager"

[The world has enough critics!]"

- And although the radiance which bares his naked Soul cannot be tainted, let him not fall short from the walnut tree

ACKNOWLEDGMENTS

The author would like to thank the following people who read and reviewed the book, or otherwise offered assistance for its generation:

Simon Haas, Teacher of yoga philosophy and author of *The Book of Dharma* and *Yoga and the Dark Night of the Soul*

Whit Hornsberger, Teacher and student of the wisdom traditions of Theravada Buddhism and classical Yoga

Ellen Johannesen, Performer, Yoga teacher and Buddhist scholar

Lizzie Hacker, Co-Director, Mahalaya Nepal

Emma Whittaker, Award winning screenwriter and author of various projects, proofreader

Jennifer Waller, Proofreader, copywriter and editor

Sido Wijga, Cover illustration *(www.sido.nl)*

Konrad Plechowski, Final editing touches

Gratitude to the wisdom that guides us all and to these wonderful contributors

ADVANCED REVIEWS

Warm, emotive, and driven towards a deep sense of union, Dylan Alexander's poetry performs a balancing act of the Soul's existence between the Earthly and the divine. There is a generosity of spirit that imbues Dylan's work. Moving between the shadow and radiance, he draws on universal symbols and ancient carriers of meaning in a gentle rhetoric that evokes homage to the likes of Rumi, Hafiz and Gibran. At once hopeful and romantic, but not without the realism of sorrow, Dylan's poetry is a heart-centered celebration of the journey. This beautiful collection is a meditation in its own right: a prayer towards an unbinding from the fetters of this world, and a continuous return to the Soul."

— Simon Haas, teacher of yoga philosophy and author of *The Book of Dharma* and *Yoga and the Dark Night of the Soul*

***

This book is epic and bold in its style. It lends imagery and vocabulary from spiritual traditions, which re-occurs throughout the book and will be familiar to those with some acquaintance with Buddhist and Hindu traditions. Dylan explains himself very well in the introduction, saying his inspired writing emerges from the point of taking a leap of faith and deciding to believe in the world, in Love, in the victory of good over bad.

This collection of poems stems from the same seed and soil. Each piece is another drop of water igniting growth and purpose. Dylan's choice of words and build up exudes a hint of "epic simplicity" giving the reader a flashlight to carry all the way through. "

— Ellen Johannesen, performer, Yoga teacher and Buddhist scholar

***

"War in The Name of Beauty is a powerful collection, with a strong sense of the poems being inspired by periods of deep contemplation. At times it feels as if the meditative process is spilling out onto the page, both compelling us to read on, and inspiring us with the courage to explore our own meditation practice more deeply. This sharing of the author's innermost journey is both very welcome and thought provoking. I found the poems both comforting and mysterious and enjoyed the rawness and power of the writing as D. S. Alexander contemplates the mysteries of the self and the power of sacred Love "

— Lizzie Hacker, Co-Director, Mahalaya Nepal

FOREWORD

The enigmatic journey of an embodied existence has fascinated the human spirit since time immemorial. As our ancient ancestors increasingly harnessed the ability to control their environment, they catalyzed a shift from an existence of being preyed upon to a Life of prayer and self-inquiry. As the surrounding environment became increasingly less threatening, our ancient brothers and sisters enabled themselves to look within and contemplating the existential meaning of this beautiful mystery called Life.

It was perhaps from that moment in time that the innate voice of the cosmos was able to be heard, finding a medium through the human vessel from which to express itself. This knowledge, previously held at bay within the walls of our precious animal bodies, incarcerated by an omnipresent fight or flight impetus, now began its march to freedom. For the first time, the teachings of the stars had an audience as the human mind began to listen; the human heart began to awaken.

It was the inherent light of knowledge (jñāna-dīptiḥ) of the universe

became illuminated within the hearts of humanity shining ceaselessly ever since within beings from all walks of Life and all corners of the planet. This innate wisdom of the stars is found within each and every one of us, and the inspiring Mr. Dylan Alexander is a living exemplar of this absolute truth.

For those of us who is fortunate enough to have come into contact with Dylan, whether on the physical plane or simply through the transformative wisdom of his words, it is undeniable that his and in turn all human lives are mediums through which this primordial wisdom is transmitted.

How blessed I am to have met Dylan upon my path. From the very first moment, I met him, the windows to his Soul revealed a luminous and compassionate presence, a Buddha-like energetic field that I am grateful to be absorbed within, each and every time we meet. As his spirit shines gracefully and beautifully, he would be the first to tell you and you will glean from the gift of his pen in this, his inspiring second book - each and every one of us is, beneath our conditioning, this pure, Buddha-nature, suffused with boundless wisdom and infinite potentiality.

May we take the time to mindfully attend to the words that have emanated from this man's heart, by way of his hand and onto the pages contained within this book. For what lies between

these two covers are a treasure trove of wisdom, stemming from the same wellspring of beatitude from which we have all sprung.

These are the teachings of each of our hearts, the collective consciousness of the cosmos. If given the time and space, these words have the power to catalyze spontaneous evolution in each of our hearts, removing the conditioned obstacles which obscure our true nature and revealing the inherent greatness within.

Thank you, Dylan, for sharing your heart, your wisdom and Life with us. We are all so blessed to be a part of your path.

Sending each and one of you infinite inspiration, patience and Love on your journey home to the refuge of your own heart.

With metta,

Whit Hornsberger • Barcelona, 2019

https://www.whithornsberger.com

PREFACE

Through my deep curiosity as a young child I've realised early on in my journey that Life holds valuable and priceless meaning. Meaning disguised within the most complex and what sometimes can be seen as the most arduous of circumstances. It is the most difficult challenges that we face, the ones that sometimes seem out of the grasp of our doing, that really force us outside of our comfort zones and allow us to transcend beyond our average thinking - or beyond our own limited capacity in which we were otherwise once stuck, and so these "cards dealt by fate", in whatever extreme and abrupt of circumstances, tend to be where the sweetest of fruits can be attained. Thus, we can say that suffering can bring man the biggest gifts of all. If only we choose to see it this way. And only when we look retrospectively we do tend to realise that in most cases a certain situation was actually the best thing that could have happened to us, bringing us to where we are in this very moment in time and space. And here we are, reading this book, in this precious moment imbued with 'nowness'. It is in this very moment of space and time where we create the power and freedom to choose our thoughts, words and actions to determine the next moment, allowing 'the next moment' to effectively become the birth of the present moment.

Life's struggles and dreams have given me a hopeful view that we all have this raw ability to rise above our own difficult and unpleasant situations and find in the midst of them our inner compass or inner voice. Intuition which is driven by a higher power. A power or a Life force present everywhere in the universe. If only we learned to tap into it and surrender.

On my journey to discover Life's meaning, I've soon realised that it is not the question (nor the answer) that is important, but rather the quality of the journey itself. Embracing life, surrendering to its ebbs and flows, and like the river learning to flow with the tides. This is a journey that I am continually learning to embrace and surrender to on my yogic path, with the support and guidance of beautiful teachers who pass down the knowledge and wisdom of yoga - an endless path that we choose to walk with heart.

This inner journey continues to shift and take on many forms reflected in my environment and people within it. I have always been fascinated by people and the choices we make. How we decide to invest time in exchange of energy, whether that be negative self-destructive thoughts, drugs, alcohol, abuse or otherwise. I've always looked up to people who make choice to be grateful. In a world where there is enough war, poverty, crime and destruction, people who choose to be grateful have given me hope that it is possible to transcend suffering - or at least to try. If we make choice to be conscious enough and be grateful despite all the suffering surrounding us, we can see the beauty and interconnectedness of Life, to feel and become Love: to be an advocate of Love. True gifts through which we inspire and uplift others. A truly beautiful way of choosing how to live Life in service to this world, of giving this shot we have on Life the very best we have: living in deepest of gratitude and fulfilment for the benefit of all.

It came naturally to me: recognising this chosen way within people struggling with their circumstances made me make my own choice to live this very way: hopeful for a better world, grateful for no matter how good or bad days may seem, and starting it all here within myself. I was going to be that person whose Life's purpose would be to find my inner peace and strength, and to give people the inspiration and hope they need in what can often seem an unfair and unjust world. A world where hope can be stronger than "poverty".

These are the essential pillars that motivate and inspire me to write freely from my heart. Unlocking the chains from my wings and giving me a creative writing style called poetic freedom, in which there are no rules or boundaries to adhere to, but rather exploration and expression of the intuitive capacity that we are all gifted with if we look beyond the dimensions of intellectual reasoning.

My ship set sail to Nepal, to the mountains, to the beautiful monastery surrounded by nature and teachers that, for me, represented just that: walking a path with heartfulness, spirit and inner peace. It was there where I started to put pen to paper for my second book. The title of this book and its nature would evolve many times, and after two years of writing in many sacred places around the world, I completed it in Dharamshala. As I set out to write, my intention was to write a book based on the two short stories from my first book, Art of The Storm. As I started to write, I heard my inner voice as loud as a thunder. Soon after, I was writing many sacred Love poems from the heart's map which was flowing through me effortlessly like a river an onto paper – a will of the universe so to speak. So here I present to you these self-reflective and meditative - and dear to my heart - sacred Love poems.

Love has no reason, no structure or rules defined by logic. As such, War in The Name of Beauty and its poetry uses poetic freedom, with intention not adhering to the principles of grammar as we know it.

Meaning that within a poem, at times, the threads of lines weaving the poem together meander from the past, through present, and to future tense. And in moments when the warrior sits in deep contemplation, poem presents rhetorical questions. This has been done purposefully, illustrating how our monkey minds travels back and forth between these four dimensions or gifts of time as we journey on the battlefield between mind and heart.

The poems reflect the trials and tribulations of a warrior and his mission in Life i.e. searching for the meaning of Life, his existential crisis, and most important and ultimate questions he holds in palms of both hands: 'Who am I?' and 'What is Love?'. Taking one of the longest journeys in the battlefield of Life, from mind to heart. And in doing so encountering some precious gifts of time: the gift associated with the past (lamentation); the gift associated with the future (anxiety of unknown), and the gift associated with the present moment (confusion); and at times transcending these states to find ultimate Love, bliss or deep current of joy which permeates the very fabric and matrix we call Universal Love. That which is the fragrance of Life itself.

12

I sincerely hope this book will give you the same inspiration and be a beacon of light on "uncharted seas", shedding hope and warmth come any season.

Here I am. At your service.

In deep gratitude.

Namaste,

Dylan

A WAR IN THE NAME OF BEAUTY

A poet is he who holds, in his tender heart, the vulnerabilities, struggle, pain, Love and compassion for all beings - encircling the mystery of the whole world

His pen is mightier than the sword

His "warrior-ship" skilled in the art of war that his sword becomes a Love poem

Living with artistry and skill: the ink that spills in battle is transformed into a song whose story will be told throughout the ages of the brave warriors

Their remembrance shedding light long after they have dissolved into the radiance of the night

Whose haunting light reaches the Soul's of those who have gracefully fallen apart

Its reflection seen by those who hold their own struggles and dream

Blinding those who do not have an open heart

Let this be *The Hero's Journey and A War in The Name of Beauty*

WAR OF LOVE

My world is breaking apart

And yet my world is falling in place

Like the shards of a shattered bowl being fixed together by golden lacquer

They say there's beauty in its complexity

Like a dagger through the dragon's heart

Beauty is in the eye of the beholder

And should such pathos be reflected in the slayer's eye on the battlefield
of Life

Let the time for the healing of wounds arrive in this war we have yet to
fight

Let me find my way in this moment as I engage in battle and bow down to
my sword

And thus, I kneel unto the vast Sky and pray not to be sheltered from the
rain but be fearless in facing my demons

Let me not be jealous of the rain or the wind

But for my heart to be open in facing my shadow and conquer my
heartbreak and misery

Let me not drown in the suffering and pain of this world and be a slave unto my worries and woes

Yet from behind my gentle smile

Let me embrace the virtue of patience so I can give the best of me in the storm of the morning light as I die another day

And I wish you the best of all the jewels the world, in its dimension, has to offer you under the shelter of the night and day

A WARRIOR'S LOVE

My determination has taken me far across the ocean seeking treasures of
the unseen kind
I've even asked the Gods: what is the purpose of my Life in this world?
But never have I come across something as precious as this
My eyes are filled with light must be blinded by the promise of this World
My heart pounds with the courage of a thousand lions
My mind is filled with dreams seemingly indestructible like a diamond
Even the Sky bows down to my sword
I'm afraid if I look away, it will all be gone

I have fought amongst the heartless singing into the night
More steel running through their veins than any empire could ever
conquer
The shadow of victory echoes in the song of the warrior's cry
For the tears are the highest expression of the sacred
Falling long before the stars have expired into the shadow of the eternal
night
Yet, the fragrance of death is a card dealt to the embassy of a free mind
Like a stainless light
My sword is a Love poet
I am its written story
Let Life be a manifestation of my wildest dreams

I have searched far above the immeasurable heavens and under the

kingdom of the sun to seek you out

I have stopped time to speak to the Universe in a silent dialogue

I even walked on the waves of the ocean

And nothing as rare did I ever find

As a warrior who walked on thorns all his Life

Did I recognize the worth of a wild flower when I crossed it's path

Silently gazing towards the sun

Like a wind extinguishing a candle and energizing a fire

There is pathos in the eye of the beholder

Because even death is permanent

And the fragrance is but a fleeting moment

Captured in the magnificence of a wild flower

Frozen in a moment of time

For what it is to let go and surrender to the tides of existence

For this hungry ghost inside fights a war in the name of beauty

To lose a wager to Love

In your service, I breathe my last breath

My devotion is as pure as gold

And like a diamond I can only be cut by a diamond

Oh, prince of thieves

You have stolen my heart

I fear I have got Nazar

From the steady gaze in your eyes

I am scarred like the Moon

I am humbled by the power of this storm

This art of mine, so worthless

I lay my sword down to your feet

This Life too belongs to you

A HUMBLE BOW

I would have followed you into the realms of the ashes

With my word, my sword and heart

A humbled bow

My "Breath-ren"

My Captain

My King

For let my suffering be meaningful if above all else

In the battlefield of War, Love and Honor

Let my tears bear witness that we have the capacity to be courageous as a

thousand strikes of a lightning bolt

Striking the heart of a warrior whose steel runs through his veins

Turning "sullen" blood into gold

For let me be an alchemist of Life above all else

With the audacity to be courageous as a thousand lions in the greatest

midst of suffering

Roaring as loud as thunder breaking up the storm cloud surrounding my

fierce heart

For in times of darkness Life questions all men

For we are not in search of the meaning of Life as so much the path and

the journey on which we have travelled none the less

So what is it that Life expects from men?

And in that contemplation lies the greatest spiritual attainment,

Does it not?

For the oil in the lamp lit by the knight of the dark Soul on a gloomy day

Allows one to see beyond himself in the darkest of hours

No matter which direction the storm howls

The mountain who in its essence remains mighty and vast like the Sky

Cannot simply bow down to the wind's magnificence

And thus let us be a sacrifice of the deepest significance

For the wild flower that blooms in the midst of adversity is the most

precious and beautiful of all

In the misty road to the passages of now

Meeting the shadow within

For that which abides within: His Soul cannot be tainted

The shadow in the light

Let it expand

HEART STORM

There's only one question on my mind

What is Life meant for me without you?

Like a dragon breathing fire

You are the air that I breathe

Like a desert longing for water

My heart longs for you

How is it possible to survive without you?

The fragrance of the night calls me to you

My heart yearns for purpose

What is my purpose without you?

Days turn into nights

Nights turn into memories and last lifetimes

But without you, days seem colder and nights seem lonely

My longing feels like centuries

So I sit and ponder under the moonlight

Whose scars are these?

The parting of the mist, yet gentle, blinds my eyes

For I cannot see beyond the veil of this Sky

Like my heart, there is just emptiness without you

Yet I see the curtain is blue

Is this the illusion that had blinded my mind?

This heart is an ocean of lost dreams

A desert of memories

A mirage of what I desire

My heart ponders who am I without you

Is this the illusion of the world standing at my feet?

What my heart wishes for always came true

So what is left to be dreamt in this small heart of mine?

What dreams are still unfilled?

What is still hiding behind the curtain?

Watching the storm passing by in the greatest Love story ever told

A heart storm is rising

I cannot see behind these eyes

But I continue to walk across this bridge from my mind to heart

To see what's on the other side

To see if you are waiting there

Even the thunderstorms cannot deter me

The lightning will light up the Sky and show me the way

Because even the Gods feels my sorrow

I neither desire pearls nor diamonds

The worldly treasure neither captures my mind

Only my heart asks you to come back to me

Who Am I?

RIVER OF LIFE

They say a heart is an ocean bed of secrets

Where the mightiest river flows

Buried scars that are as deep as the river

Creating It's own dreams and journey to return to the source of creation

Conquering and destroying anything that stands in its path

The river is the lemniscus power of creation by willpower and desire

The path of the brave heart

Drawing divine power down from the heavens into its sacred valleys

Where there is water there is Life

Settlements amongst the riverbank and rushing brooks

Offerings of the saints and sinners

History carved in the fabled sands of time

The river flows through the strongest mountains creating its own path

Even if it is split in half the river will find a way to return to the ocean

On the path of this river of Life...

I have been a seeker of Love under the kingdom of the Heavens

I have been a warrior in The Art of The Storm

A spiritual pilgrim in The Art of War

An Alchemist in The Law of Divine Compensation

I have become an immortal reflection of the river of eternal Life

Which ebbs and flows on its sacred journey towards the heart of the ocean

Where the crest of the wave returns back into the water from which it was

manifested

The bond between the river joining by the ocean

Is likened to a sword that defends an empire

Where the river flows

Order surely follows

A prayer the sword stays strong in combat in the battlefield of Life

Where Life and death are *one*

BOUNDLESS (SATYA)

Since I found myself in the reflection of Life's greatest adventures

I vanquished misery

Neither tied to any vow

Nor shadowed by any boundaries that once set foot on this throne like a

sun falling towards the pilgrimage to the east

This heart of mine has taken flight and peers above the highest mountain

on Earth

It ventures across the vast kingdom that the rays of the sun falls upon

As it rises from the horizon of the Western Ghats

Only living in this moment, I fear nothing

There is only desire to soar high above the valley of the kings and queens

Where the cycle of birth and death is a timeless spirit

I once again have desire to live unmasked

In this moment, I have died and flourished a thousand times

I have surrendered my body and mind to the ways of the warrior

A path less travelled shadowed by doubt of the frivolous minds

I have pledged my heart to the discerning sword

A weapon striking fear in the pounding veins of the blind where

permanence has consumed him gravely

Breaking through the chains of ignorance, fear, karma and emotions that

my spirit once was enslaved unto

I bow down to the Love that has set this Soul on fire between the fine lines

of fate and destiny

There is nothing I have achieved that has not already been written by the
almighty hand
There is a higher wisdom at play that the gaze of this eye cannot capture
Or can any treasures buried deep beneath the mine of rubies match in
unparalleled power

This intoxication is like a wild storm
With the power to conquer any demon
Destroying everything built on its path
Before the world was elusive and darker than I could ever understand
I do not recognize this place any more
After coming out of the darkness
There is only the scent of the forest I can see
It has the Midas touch that quiets me
Like the golden petals of a wild flower in bloom
Facing North towards the glorious sun
A heart as courageous as lions that cannot be tamed
Boundless is this heart beyond the vanquished temples
Like the sky which has no shadow of doubt or color of illusion

UNINVITED LOVE

With this uninvited Love my sadness and sorrows are withered like the
autumn leaves meeting in the winter grace
With this uninvited Love my weakness and despair transformed like the
spring buds blossoming under the summer's rays

I always wished for perfection in Love
For Love to be the personification of Love itself
And Love to forgive all my weaknesses and cradle them like the night
cradles the day with no judgement
My daydream turned into admiration
In my infatuation I held a seed in my heart that bloomed into a rosebud
The color so red my mind has been tainted
The sweetest little thing you have ever seen growing in a dream With a
spirit that felt so inviting

I've learnt to be the man in Life who we can depend on
A shoulder in the storm, when Life gets so crazy, for us to lean on
I would Love the mountain and heavens
Just as I Love the ground that you walk on
Don't you know...
Only for you, I would crush any sorrows and give you the world in a
heartbeat

My heart is more tranquil than the vast Sky that you look upon

My eyes are deeper than the ocean together we set sail on

And when you say my eyes are beautiful

It's because they are looking at an uninvited Love

My breath speaks a truth only for you

In my mind, there's a forest where pure beauty remains

And beyond the pine trees there I'm waiting for you

Love is pure silence

Silence is gold

No strength can carry the weight of the gold that I hold in my heart

I gave up my wings just for you

I fell from the heaven and onto this Earth

Finding my place on this journey in the art of this Life

At times it was hard I tried to erase myself from the picture

And at times I was bruised I wished the wind would hide all my flaws

behind the branches of the trees

But I fell so hard that I fell in Love

With this uninvited Love my despair fell like snow in the dessert

I Love you like the Moon Loves the sun

Just for you I would be the perfect man with the qualities which personify

Love itself

So a perfection in a Love exist in this world

That I would be able to hand it to you on a silver platter

And when I whisper I Love you

Your heart will awaken and walk through the path of fire just to be with

mine

There's no sadness

No you and me

Even I can't seem to understand this uninvited Love

I was never a man to give up on Life

Never a man to give up on dreaming

I learnt to be the man we can depend on

All the sorrows the fears and all the tears prepared me to be the man I have become today

To read between the lines of real Love and a dream that kept me longing in the wilderness

Now I'm so naked so bare

I have nothing to give to this universe but my undressed heart and naked Soul

All I ask is you hold it in your hands and protect it from the shadow of the clouds

Because this storm has brought an unexpected visitor

A gift of an uninvited Love

WONDERS OF THE MONSOON

The world has come to see me dance

And the clouds have started to thunder

Even the shower has captured my heart

No hurricane or lightning can extinguish my desire

The gravity of the Moon compared to Earth is strong today and the tides

have become restless like my mind

My heart is searching for an answer

There is neither reason nor rhyme

Why I feel so elated

The monsoon has caught me under a spell and set this aching heart on fire

Let's dance in this pouring rain

I hear the voice of the rain

Sing with the rhythm of my heart beat

I'm drowned in Love and lost my mind

My thirst is quenched

This crazy heart of mine seems unaware of the world and neither claims

its worldly treasures

My eyes are tainted waiting to see you in the falling rain

My mind is restless

There is neither reason nor rhyme

Today the monsoon has caught me off guard

I can barely speak

The stars above are silver shadows

Dancing in the rain

There I see you shining

Smiling, dancing, swaying

Whose footsteps are these?

Who is the beholder of this gaze?

Who knocks on the door of my heart?

At the crossroads of my Life

This is the season of Love

The monsoon has stolen my heart

Meeting my beLoved in the monsoon rain

I am burning bright in this thunderous cloud scorching through the

shallow skies

You are the king of dreams

I'm the prince of thieves

The queen has conquered

My ego is captured

I'm unchained and drenched in this rain

The atmosphere has taken hold

I'm intoxicated by the spirit of the rain

Neither the air can blow my fears away nor the fire consume my sorrow

But the rain soothes my heart

The lamp in my heart glows fiercely

Burning every cell of my body

Even a gust of wind cannot blow away the light through which I see my

reflection in every drop of nectar that falls from the abode of the Gods

And the birds they sing from the thunderous Sky

I have searched and searched everywhere for you
I even walked on fire and on every cloud to find you
In the rain, I see my Soul

INTOXICATED

Even the Goddess descended her throne to slay the king demon

So, what small sacrifice is it for me to cross this ocean to Love?

She is the beLoved essence of the universe

Graceful like a deer

The radiance of a thousand Moons

Jai Shree Radharani

Whose are these footsteps walking towards me?

Who is this knocking on the doorways of my heart?

A Goddess has landed on Earth

And her spirit intoxicates me

Jai Shree Gayatri

Even the king has turned into a madman

The streets are singing loudly

Everyone is drunk in Love and her spirits has taken us by the heels to the secret abode of the Goddess

In the secret chambers of her heart

Even common people have a place to rejoice

In the land of kings and queens

Jai Shree Parvati

Without the eternal

I fear the sea in the storm

Without the Kingdom of heaven

I fear a night with no Moon

For she has brought us salvation

She is the Moon

Without the Goddess

I fear I will lose my way

She has come to bring us redemption

Jai Shree Saraswati

Since I have become intoxicated with Love

I have become free

Like a sword of a warrior

The tale of my Love will echo through the centuries

In the greatest Love story ever told

But moments are fleeting

And fleeting moments are history

So, I will embrace this moment and live for a thousand nights

Jai Jai Kali Mata

The world says I am crazy

Maybe they're right

But I will rejoice and sing into the night

Like a flower, so delicate, yet my heart is open in full bloom

Blossoming under the candlelight of the Moon

And this wildflower will forgive the ones who stepped on it and crushed its dreams

All I have to offer you is my sweet scent

Jai Jai Durga Ma

I am gazing upon the beardless man and wear Nazar

To protect me against the evil eye

You have wounded me with your poisonous arrow

And I have become intoxicated with Love

They say I am crazy and maybe they are right

But I crossed the ocean and the seven seas

And I have found refuge in no-man's land

I have become one

I found my spirit under the sun

Kissed by the Moon

My heart is illuminated

Like a parachute I have no fear

Your name is a soothing balm

She has come to slay the demon

She has come

Sita Sita Ram

She is the field of pure light

There is nothing else I can think of

She is the embodiment of yoga

My shackles have been lifted

My human spirit humbled

The Goddess descends from her abode to slay the evil demon

So what price is it for me to pay?

To lay my armour and climb this mountain

And dance freely into the night

They say I have gone crazy

But even today the king turns into a madman

And the streets rejoice with light

Because she has come to give us redemption

Jai Shree Laxmi

I am intoxicated with Love

My Love is in motion

The sun has set on our adventures

But our story continues on into the night

I am one

I have become one

BEYOND

What is it to be?

And become?

With the divine mathematical precision of the universe

Like the golden ratio which governs the natural order of space and time

To unfold into the beauty of your becoming

To naturally exist in the splendor of this moment

In all its glory

Radiant like gold purified by the alchemist touch

Beyond that which any reflection can bear witness to

In the wellspring of Joy

This which holds the most potent gifts of the three wise kings:

Satya, Prem, Roop

The pure and regal qualities of a deer

Preserved in the amber of nature's greatest moments

Hidden behind the scent of the forest

Or even the bravest of smiles

Pure is of the essence of the brave heart

Who accepts his destiny and lives in the simplest of moments

Treasuring the present moment as the ultimate gift to mankind

In the crevices of the deep mines

Where mineral gases inject and precipitate over thousands of years

The river of stillness is inviting beyond measure of experience and depth of time

Like the silver face of a blade of a knife

Both sides have potential for good and for destruction

The balance between Namarupa

Resting on the fine line between a jagged edge sword

Slicing through the sound of thunder into tiny fragments of hopes and possibilities

Opening up one vision to an awe-inspiring field of Consciousness

Awe struck by a lightning bolt

Such is the gaze of the miner

Who first lays his eyes on an Earthly masterpiece

Within the deep buried mines

Where the world's greatest minerals are awaiting to be discovered

Beyond dualism of momentary pleasures and fleeting moments

A world beyond worlds

A world beyond measure

A world beyond appearances

Within the cave of your heart's mind

Is what has been calling your name

Towards the river of your Soul

A secret whisper to the initiated

Unravelling in the mystery of the Universe

Powerful reminders of the divine Consciousness revealed

The real beauty of gratitude

Is in the eye of the beholder

A beggar, a miner or a master

UNBREAKABLE

When the world is dark

And you're consumed with grief

When the Sky is grey and cold

With no end in sight

When you're feeling is small like a feather

Winter comes and thunder hails

With promise of rain to quench your thirst

There's a deeper meaning behind the storm

If you watch gracefully upon the silent hill

The lightning will light up the Sky

So you can see your journey unfold

It's so very special

The seedling breaks through the fruit stone contained within its shell

To become free and unbound from the darkness, it was encircled in

And so too must spontaneous wisdom arise through the breaking of your

pain

Buried deep beneath the gravel of knowledge

What is the fine line between Life and death

The space between your inhale and exhale

Stimulus and response

Fate and destiny?

A field of conscious unmanifest under the spirit of the sun

Come too close and this too shall burn you to ashes

The spiritual pilgrim who sits in awe under the spirit of the sun

Wondering silently

Dances in the miracle of Life's greatest mystery

Unchained by the scales of the season

Unbound by the nine astronomical planets

UnEarthed and placated by the stars

The ocean is a desert of longing

An oasis of self-fulfilling prophecy

The poison of samsara will have you fooled for liquor to sweeten your

taste buds for momentary pleasure

For the seeker of glorification and power

Will be knighted into a cycle of pain

For the seeker of Love and unity

Will be knighted into an eternal bliss

He will break through pain that once consumed him gravely

And peer delicately above the ground

Weathered by the elements

Unbound and unbreakable

Like a rainbow

Glorious under the Sky

Holding his pain in the palm of his hands

As a gentle offering

Bathed in the sacred splendor of joy, delight and sorrow

And the poison that surround your heart

Dissolve into the radiance of the visiting storm

That washes over your field and lights up the landscape of your heart

So compassion can shine through and heal the child within

Then you too shall experience the kingdom of heaven within

And choose to be an ambassador of Love

A beacon of light in someone's darkest hour of need

This too is the law of nature

And this too shall pass

ME AND MY SHADOW

I'm looking through the window waiting for the paint to dry

What I see you don't see

Sometimes it's like a tornado

Sometimes it's like a waterfall

If only you can imagine what it's really like

But then again my pen can show you what it means to feel like

A thunder cloud

A rainbow in somebody else's cloud

Right now there's a lightning bolt in my chest creating a heart storm

It's raining heavily and I can barely see

With a knife in my chest I can barely breathe

But with blood of steel

I have more thunder running through my veins to continue this fight

There's enough war in the world to keep your eyes from bleeding

Enough greed to keep your mind from feeling

As long as the world keeps the wrong in sight

It's like I'm in flight

A bird with two wings

Enough miseducation and hatred to keep you from drowning

But Life resuscitates me

I guess I don't know my own strength

Do you ever watch the news?

Have you ever seen somebody drop dead?

Have you ever lost somebody you Love so much?

You can barely breathe and Life feels cold

And you're lost in grief and the world all of a sudden feels like you're

going insane

Feels like Life is over and you wonder whether it will take you under

Take a breath

Count to ten and start again

Then you take a glimpse into time

And suddenly you feel free

A message from above

A saving grace

Or so it feels

And the pain you hold so dearly

Reckons you to be present in the now

Living for today

With no tomorrow in mind

And yesterday out of plain sight

And in this moment you realize your purpose or what it's meant to be

A soldier in your own kingdom

To protect the weak and keep the heartless at bay

An ambassador of Love

To free the wingless Soul's that have been trapped in cages

Sometimes I'm lost in moments

And the clouds take over

I guess sometimes no one really knows you and you feel so alone

Even these moments feel like they are slipping through your fingers

And yesterday feels like it's lost in the sand of time

Looking out the window and Life flashes before you

And all you have is this moment

But even then

This moment is hard to grasp onto

If only you knew

This moment is still an illusion created through the window pane

Only a reflection

It's just a matter of perspective

ME AND MY SHADOW PT. 2 (SANDS OF TIME)

Sometimes I wonder if we could turn back the hands of time

Turn the hour glass frame around

And watch the sand dripping down the walls

Can we go back and reverse the things we said

Things we should have done or things we should have said

Isn't this the biggest cause of suffering?

Wanting something to happen that doesn't really exist

Because even when this sentence ends

It will all be a dream in the end

So Life continues falling back into the same old patterns

Same routines

Same games

Almost feels like you're on a hamster wheel

And when you step off for a moment

And catch your breath

You understand you're the same as me

No separation

No distinction

No you and me

Because when you label things you will no longer see

And in the end beneath the flesh and bones they say all we are is Love

But do we really know what this is?

And so I question everything that has come to be

And so it seems to all appearances he is a fool

A self portrait of a dreamer

A fool yesterday

A king today

A forgotten memory tomorrow

REFLECTIONS OF A LOTUS FLOWER

Whose whispers of Love are these?

Who is this unexpected visitor that arrived at the crossroad's of my Life?

Shattered my world into a thousand pieces

And coloured by Life with a thousand emotions

What is your name?

What is this form?

All I see is a shadow

A fragrance that even my heart cannot detect

You have taken the dagger out of my heart

And healed my bleeding wound with your touch

Your name is a soothing balm to my heart

No Moon can hide the scar of my affection

Which has illuminated my heart and mind

No darkness can dim this light

Which has embraced the sadness and held it up high above the Sky to the Gods

Not even the world's most beautiful treasure can steal the thunder from my eyes

They are beautiful because they have been silently looking for you in wonder in the darkest of days

Today I am like a lotus flower

I have grown from the murkiest waters of this lake

Floating on the surface in full bloom

Untainted from the mud from which I emerged

I buried this sadness of mine deep beneath the soil

I even faced all the problems of mine and embraced the thorns with

compassion

Today neither water can rest on my leaves

Nor can I deny myself of the sun's ray

But I too shall be caressed by the water drops as they roll off my petals to

fall back into the lake and become water again

I've been sitting for a thousand years silently in awe upon this lake

And praying in a silent dialogue with God

With both hands together I've asked for you to pick me out from the

muddy waters

And in the reflection of the lake I've seen you for a moment

My prayers seem to have been answered

If even for just a moment

This too is a brief window into my Soul

The radiance of the soft morning peeks into my Soul

Quenches my thirst and drowns my sorrows

There's a question on my mind

Who is this shadow that has captured my heart?

Like a poisonous arrow shot directly towards my heart and dissolved into

flowers

My world is infected by this scent

And the sweetest poison is flowing through my veins once again

Who is this Love that is mirroring me?

My spirit has been awoken

I have become crazy in Love

But it seems the rest of the world is still sleeping

Or maybe I am just dreaming

My world has become intoxicated

I am like a flame

But how can this flame survive when it is smothered with smoke?

PRINCE OF DEATH

Isn't it funny, the many masks we wear

Moving from a to z, living like a catastrophe from behind our hollow lives

Now isn't this the state of mankind?

Looking in the mirror seeing a reflection

Feeling ourselves with lies

Feeding ourselves with strangers passing by

Trying to be on time

We walk around with frozen smiles

Only to forget our hearts, forget our needs and fill ourselves with fantasies

We think, we believe

Feel sorrow and grief

And fill our mind with hollow lies

We pick words as we go

And every time we take the bait

We follow riches and feed ourselves with wanting more

Feed our demons and sharpening our claws

Consumed with greed and frozen smiles

We walk parallel lives

Your eyes in the mirror look under the pillow

It must be that old evil spirit slowing you down into the ground

Look behind you and the prince of death awaits all mankind

FIND YOUR WAY BACK

Weep dear child

For in your tears there is a transformation

Let yourself be fully embodied and surrender to the eternal wisdom

The Earth will carry your burden and carry your tears to the boundless
ocean

Don't let your feet be troubled dear friend

Keep on walking on your path for each sacred step you take, I will carry
your weight and walk with you

Is this a path less travelled or a traveler on his path?

Either way, don't confuse yourself with Love and regret

Because the profuse insanity of mankind is dwelling upon the effect

Where cause is a vanquished misery

Lost in the cage of a thief

Who stole his time and emptied his pockets

Blinded by the veil of delusion

Open your heart freely and reach out to the universe

Hold each spirit of breath in the sacred fragments of hope

For gravity is a gift to mankind

Tied in the contraction of the human psyche

Relax unto the tides of existence

And I will be guiding you fruitfully

On your journey to the point of no existence

Here you can inhale and start again

REFLECTION

The light of the full Moon refracted into my dark side

Raises the vibration of my heart rate

The second-hand reflection in the mirror

Has me thinking

Whose thoughts are these?

The apparition of my shadow reflected

Whose image is this?

Is this the dark side of Love I see?

What is the source of this light?

Is this Love that I feel?

The potential which cannot be reflected in the mirror?

My world has turned upside down

The nectar of the Moon is consuming the sun

Giving me power to rise over the realms of fear

And choose between the fine lines of fate and destiny

Between the gates of heaven and hell

Is this the land of the free will?

The power to choose to spread my wings

Unchained from the shackles that kept me prisoner from the church of the

"free folk"

And rise not into temptation but into the expansiveness we call freedom

To wear a uniform of the free-spirited

To become a poet of a free mind

Vanquished from knowing my reflection

When the shadow falls and the sun rises

I become a conqueror of the mountains

A mighty Soul unarmored

Taking a sacred pilgrimage

From mind to heart

Finding beauty is the Gods handwriting

In the present meaning of time

THE BEGINNING OF THE END

The fallen warrior withdrew the long silver-tainted blade from his pumping heart

For in the briefest of moment, he caught in the sword's reflection a tiny glimpse of the raw nakedness and purest expressions of his Soul

He was in awe of the sword's potential which magnificently captured the beauty that shone bright like the brilliance of the snow-capped reflective Moon of Saturn

Until he closes his eyes into the realm of this existence, and shadow fell upon his hour

The hermit lowers his hood and asks the brave warrior

What power does the shadow have before the sun?

What power does the sun have before the Moon?

What power does the Moon have before the ocean?

What power does the ocean have upon mankind?

What power does mankind have upon inner peace?

What is inner peace in the midst of war and suffering?

THE PATH OF THE WARRIOR

The spiritual path of the warrior is not an easy road to take

It requires strength of mind and will power [discipline and discernment]

Skillful endurance and patience in equal measures

Sthira Sukha [steadiness/balance & harmony/comfort]:

Strength to bow down and stand in awe of the cosmos which we have been catapulted into at great force and speed

... and to accept how powerful you truly are and can be, beyond measure and time!